GRATITUDE JOURNAL

This journal belongs to:

Joyful Journals

Day: _____   Date: ___/___/_____

TODAY, I AM GRATEFUL FOR...

AWESOME THINGS THAT HAPPENED TODAY...

Day: _____   Date: ____/____/_____

TODAY, I AM GRATEFUL FOR...

_____

_____

_____

_____

_____

_____

_____

AWESOME THINGS THAT HAPPENED TODAY...

_____

_____

_____

_____

_____

_____

_____

Day: _____   Date: ____/____/_____

TODAY, I AM GRATEFUL FOR...

_____

_____

_____

_____

_____

_____

AWESOME THINGS THAT HAPPENED TODAY...

_____

_____

_____

_____

_____

_____

_____

Day: _____   Date: ____/____/_____

TODAY, I AM GRATEFUL FOR...

_____

_____

_____

_____

_____

_____

_____

AWESOME THINGS THAT HAPPENED TODAY...

_____

_____

_____

_____

_____

_____

_____

Day: _____   Date: ____/____/_____

TODAY, I AM GRATEFUL FOR...

_____

_____

_____

_____

_____

_____

AWESOME THINGS THAT HAPPENED TODAY...

_____

_____

_____

_____

_____

_____

Day: _____   Date: ____/____/_____

TODAY, I AM GRATEFUL FOR...

_____
_____
_____
_____
_____
_____
_____
_____

AWESOME THINGS THAT HAPPENED TODAY...

_____
_____
_____
_____
_____
_____
_____
_____

Day: _____   Date: ____/____/_____

TODAY, I AM GRATEFUL FOR...

_____

_____

_____

_____

_____

_____

AWESOME THINGS THAT HAPPENED TODAY...

_____

_____

_____

_____

_____

_____

_____

Day: _____   Date: ____/____/_____

TODAY, I AM GRATEFUL FOR...

_____

_____

_____

_____

_____

_____

_____

AWESOME THINGS THAT HAPPENED TODAY...

_____

_____

_____

_____

_____

_____

_____

Day: _____   Date: ____/____/_____

TODAY, I AM GRATEFUL FOR...

_____

_____

_____

_____

_____

_____

AWESOME THINGS THAT HAPPENED TODAY...

_____

_____

_____

_____

_____

_____

_____

Day: _____   Date: ____/____/_____

TODAY, I AM GRATEFUL FOR...

_____

_____

_____

_____

_____

_____

_____

AWESOME THINGS THAT HAPPENED TODAY...

_____

_____

_____

_____

_____

_____

_____

Day: _____   Date: ___/___/_____

TODAY, I AM GRATEFUL FOR...

_____

_____

_____

_____

_____

_____

_____

AWESOME THINGS THAT HAPPENED TODAY...

_____

_____

_____

_____

_____

_____

_____

Day: _____   Date: ___/___/_____

TODAY, I AM GRATEFUL FOR...

_____
_____
_____
_____
_____
_____
_____

AWESOME THINGS THAT HAPPENED TODAY...

_____
_____
_____
_____
_____
_____
_____

Day: _____   Date: ____/____/_____

TODAY, I AM GRATEFUL FOR...

_____

_____

_____

_____

_____

_____

AWESOME THINGS THAT HAPPENED TODAY...

_____

_____

_____

_____

_____

_____

Day: _____   Date: ____/____/_____

TODAY, I AM GRATEFUL FOR...

_____

_____

_____

_____

_____

_____

_____

AWESOME THINGS THAT HAPPENED TODAY...

_____

_____

_____

_____

_____

_____

_____

Day: _____   Date: ___/___/_____

TODAY, I AM GRATEFUL FOR...

_____

_____

_____

_____

_____

_____

AWESOME THINGS THAT HAPPENED TODAY...

_____

_____

_____

_____

_____

_____

Day: _____ Date: ___/___/_____

TODAY, I AM GRATEFUL FOR...

_____
_____
_____
_____
_____
_____
_____

AWESOME THINGS THAT HAPPENED TODAY...

_____
_____
_____
_____
_____
_____
_____

Day: _____   Date: ___/___/_____

TODAY, I AM GRATEFUL FOR...

_____

_____

_____

_____

_____

_____

AWESOME THINGS THAT HAPPENED TODAY...

_____

_____

_____

_____

_____

_____

_____

Day: _____   Date: ___/___/_____

TODAY, I AM GRATEFUL FOR...

_____

_____

_____

_____

_____

_____

_____

AWESOME THINGS THAT HAPPENED TODAY...

_____

_____

_____

_____

_____

_____

_____

Day: _____   Date: ___/___/_____

TODAY, I AM GRATEFUL FOR...

_____

_____

_____

_____

_____

_____

AWESOME THINGS THAT HAPPENED TODAY...

_____

_____

_____

_____

_____

_____

_____

Day: _____   Date: ___/___/_____

TODAY, I AM GRATEFUL FOR...

_____
_____
_____
_____
_____
_____
_____

AWESOME THINGS THAT HAPPENED TODAY...

_____
_____
_____
_____
_____
_____
_____

Day: _____   Date: ____/____/_____

TODAY, I AM GRATEFUL FOR...

_____

_____

_____

_____

_____

_____

AWESOME THINGS THAT HAPPENED TODAY...

_____

_____

_____

_____

_____

_____

Day: _____   Date: ___/___/_____

TODAY, I AM GRATEFUL FOR...

_____

_____

_____

_____

_____

_____

AWESOME THINGS THAT HAPPENED TODAY...

_____

_____

_____

_____

_____

_____

Day: _____   Date: ____/____/_____

TODAY, I AM GRATEFUL FOR...

_____

_____

_____

_____

_____

AWESOME THINGS THAT HAPPENED TODAY...

_____

_____

_____

_____

_____

_____

Day: _____   Date: ___/___/_____

TODAY, I AM GRATEFUL FOR...

_____

_____

_____

_____

_____

_____

AWESOME THINGS THAT HAPPENED TODAY...

_____

_____

_____

_____

_____

_____

Day: _____   Date: ___/___/_____

TODAY, I AM GRATEFUL FOR...

_____

_____

_____

_____

_____

_____

_____

AWESOME THINGS THAT HAPPENED TODAY...

_____

_____

_____

_____

_____

_____

_____

Day: _____   Date: ____/____/_____

TODAY, I AM GRATEFUL FOR...

_____
_____
_____
_____
_____
_____
_____

AWESOME THINGS THAT HAPPENED TODAY...

_____
_____
_____
_____
_____
_____
_____

Day: _____   Date: ____/____/_____

TODAY, I AM GRATEFUL FOR...

_____

_____

_____

_____

_____

_____

AWESOME THINGS THAT HAPPENED TODAY...

_____

_____

_____

_____

_____

_____

Day: _____   Date: ___/___/_____

TODAY, I AM GRATEFUL FOR...

_____

_____

_____

_____

_____

_____

AWESOME THINGS THAT HAPPENED TODAY...

_____

_____

_____

_____

_____

_____

Day: _____   Date: ____/____/_____

TODAY, I AM GRATEFUL FOR...

_____

_____

_____

_____

_____

_____

AWESOME THINGS THAT HAPPENED TODAY...

_____

_____

_____

_____

_____

_____

_____

Day: _____   Date: ___/___/_____

TODAY, I AM GRATEFUL FOR...

_____
_____
_____
_____
_____
_____
_____
_____

AWESOME THINGS THAT HAPPENED TODAY...

_____
_____
_____
_____
_____
_____
_____

Day: _____   Date: ____/____/_____

TODAY, I AM GRATEFUL FOR...

_____

_____

_____

_____

_____

_____

AWESOME THINGS THAT HAPPENED TODAY...

_____

_____

_____

_____

_____

_____

_____

Day: _____   Date: ____/____/_____

TODAY, I AM GRATEFUL FOR...

_____

_____

_____

_____

_____

_____

_____

AWESOME THINGS THAT HAPPENED TODAY...

_____

_____

_____

_____

_____

_____

_____

Day: _____   Date: ___/___/_____

TODAY, I AM GRATEFUL FOR...

_____

_____

_____

_____

_____

_____

AWESOME THINGS THAT HAPPENED TODAY...

_____

_____

_____

_____

_____

_____

_____

Day: _____   Date: ____/____/_____

TODAY, I AM GRATEFUL FOR...

_____
_____
_____
_____
_____
_____
_____

AWESOME THINGS THAT HAPPENED TODAY...

_____
_____
_____
_____
_____
_____
_____

Day: _____   Date: ___/___/_____

TODAY, I AM GRATEFUL FOR...

_____
_____
_____
_____
_____
_____
_____

AWESOME THINGS THAT HAPPENED TODAY...

_____
_____
_____
_____
_____
_____
_____

Day: _____   Date: ___/___/_____

TODAY, I AM GRATEFUL FOR...

_____
_____
_____
_____
_____
_____
_____
_____

AWESOME THINGS THAT HAPPENED TODAY...

_____
_____
_____
_____
_____
_____
_____

Day: _____   Date: ___/___/_____

TODAY, I AM GRATEFUL FOR...

_____
_____
_____
_____
_____
_____
_____

AWESOME THINGS THAT HAPPENED TODAY...

_____
_____
_____
_____
_____
_____
_____

Day: _____   Date: ____/____/_____

TODAY, I AM GRATEFUL FOR...

_____

_____

_____

_____

_____

_____

AWESOME THINGS THAT HAPPENED TODAY...

_____

_____

_____

_____

_____

_____

_____

Day: _____   Date: ___/___/_____

TODAY, I AM GRATEFUL FOR...

_____
_____
_____
_____
_____
_____

AWESOME THINGS THAT HAPPENED TODAY...

_____
_____
_____
_____
_____
_____
_____

Day: _____   Date: ___/___/_____

TODAY, I AM GRATEFUL FOR...

_____
_____
_____
_____
_____
_____

AWESOME THINGS THAT HAPPENED TODAY...

_____
_____
_____
_____
_____
_____

Day: _____   Date: ___/___/_____

TODAY, I AM GRATEFUL FOR...

_____

_____

_____

_____

_____

_____

AWESOME THINGS THAT HAPPENED TODAY...

_____

_____

_____

_____

_____

_____

Day: _____   Date: ___/___/_____

TODAY, I AM GRATEFUL FOR...

_____

_____

_____

_____

_____

_____

AWESOME THINGS THAT HAPPENED TODAY...

_____

_____

_____

_____

_____

_____

_____

Day: _____   Date: ____/____/_____

TODAY, I AM GRATEFUL FOR...

_____

_____

_____

_____

_____

_____

AWESOME THINGS THAT HAPPENED TODAY...

_____

_____

_____

_____

_____

_____

Day: _____   Date: ____/____/_____

TODAY, I AM GRATEFUL FOR...

_____

_____

_____

_____

_____

_____

_____

_____

AWESOME THINGS THAT HAPPENED TODAY...

_____

_____

_____

_____

_____

_____

_____

_____

Day: _____   Date: ___/___/_____

TODAY, I AM GRATEFUL FOR...

_____

_____

_____

_____

_____

_____

AWESOME THINGS THAT HAPPENED TODAY...

_____

_____

_____

_____

_____

_____

Day: _____   Date: ____/____/_____

TODAY, I AM GRATEFUL FOR...

_____
_____
_____
_____
_____
_____
_____

AWESOME THINGS THAT HAPPENED TODAY...

_____
_____
_____
_____
_____
_____

Day: _____   Date: ____/____/_____

TODAY, I AM GRATEFUL FOR...

_____

_____

_____

_____

_____

_____

AWESOME THINGS THAT HAPPENED TODAY...

_____

_____

_____

_____

_____

_____

Day: _____   Date: ___/___/_____

TODAY, I AM GRATEFUL FOR...

_____

_____

_____

_____

_____

_____

AWESOME THINGS THAT HAPPENED TODAY...

_____

_____

_____

_____

_____

_____

_____

Day: _____   Date: ____/____/_____

TODAY, I AM GRATEFUL FOR...

AWESOME THINGS THAT HAPPENED TODAY...

Day: _____   Date: ____/____/_____

TODAY, I AM GRATEFUL FOR...

_____

_____

_____

_____

_____

_____

_____

_____

AWESOME THINGS THAT HAPPENED TODAY...

_____

_____

_____

_____

_____

_____

_____

_____

Day: _____   Date: ____/____/_____

TODAY, I AM GRATEFUL FOR...

_____

_____

_____

_____

_____

_____

_____

AWESOME THINGS THAT HAPPENED TODAY...

_____

_____

_____

_____

_____

_____

_____

_____

Day: _____   Date: ____/____/_____

TODAY, I AM GRATEFUL FOR...

_____
_____
_____
_____
_____
_____
_____
_____

AWESOME THINGS THAT HAPPENED TODAY...

_____
_____
_____
_____
_____
_____
_____
_____

Day: _____   Date: ____/____/_____

TODAY, I AM GRATEFUL FOR...

_____

_____

_____

_____

_____

_____

AWESOME THINGS THAT HAPPENED TODAY...

_____

_____

_____

_____

_____

_____

Day: _____   Date: ___/___/_____

TODAY, I AM GRATEFUL FOR...

_____
_____
_____
_____
_____
_____
_____

AWESOME THINGS THAT HAPPENED TODAY...

_____
_____
_____
_____
_____
_____
_____

Day: _____   Date: ____/____/_____

TODAY, I AM GRATEFUL FOR...

_____

_____

_____

_____

_____

_____

AWESOME THINGS THAT HAPPENED TODAY...

_____

_____

_____

_____

_____

_____

_____

Day: _____ Date: ___/___/_____

TODAY, I AM GRATEFUL FOR...

_____

_____

_____

_____

_____

_____

AWESOME THINGS THAT HAPPENED TODAY...

_____

_____

_____

_____

_____

_____

Day: _____   Date: ___/___/_____

TODAY, I AM GRATEFUL FOR...

_____

_____

_____

_____

_____

_____

AWESOME THINGS THAT HAPPENED TODAY...

_____

_____

_____

_____

_____

_____

Day: _____   Date: ____/____/_____

TODAY, I AM GRATEFUL FOR...

_____

_____

_____

_____

_____

_____

_____

AWESOME THINGS THAT HAPPENED TODAY...

_____

_____

_____

_____

_____

_____

_____

Day: _____   Date: ____/____/_____

TODAY, I AM GRATEFUL FOR...

_____

_____

_____

_____

_____

_____

_____

AWESOME THINGS THAT HAPPENED TODAY...

_____

_____

_____

_____

_____

_____

_____

Day: _____   Date: ___/___/_____

TODAY, I AM GRATEFUL FOR...

_____
_____
_____
_____
_____
_____
_____

AWESOME THINGS THAT HAPPENED TODAY...

_____
_____
_____
_____
_____
_____
_____

Day: _____   Date: ___/___/_____

TODAY, I AM GRATEFUL FOR...

_____

_____

_____

_____

_____

_____

_____

AWESOME THINGS THAT HAPPENED TODAY...

_____

_____

_____

_____

_____

_____

_____

Day: _____   Date: ____/____/_____

TODAY, I AM GRATEFUL FOR...

_____

_____

_____

_____

_____

_____

_____

AWESOME THINGS THAT HAPPENED TODAY...

_____

_____

_____

_____

_____

_____

_____

Day: _____   Date: ____/____/_____

TODAY, I AM GRATEFUL FOR...

_____
_____
_____
_____
_____
_____

AWESOME THINGS THAT HAPPENED TODAY...

_____
_____
_____
_____
_____
_____

Day: _____   Date: ___/___/_____

TODAY, I AM GRATEFUL FOR...

_____
_____
_____
_____
_____
_____
_____
_____

AWESOME THINGS THAT HAPPENED TODAY...

_____
_____
_____
_____
_____
_____
_____
_____

Day: _____   Date: ____/____/_____

TODAY, I AM GRATEFUL FOR...

_____

_____

_____

_____

_____

_____

_____

AWESOME THINGS THAT HAPPENED TODAY...

_____

_____

_____

_____

_____

_____

_____

Day: _____   Date: ____/____/_____

TODAY, I AM GRATEFUL FOR...

_____
_____
_____
_____
_____
_____
_____

AWESOME THINGS THAT HAPPENED TODAY...

_____
_____
_____
_____
_____
_____

Day: _____ Date: ___/___/_____

TODAY, I AM GRATEFUL FOR...

AWESOME THINGS THAT HAPPENED TODAY...

Day: _____   Date: ____/____/_____

TODAY, I AM GRATEFUL FOR...

_____
_____
_____
_____
_____
_____
_____

AWESOME THINGS THAT HAPPENED TODAY...

_____
_____
_____
_____
_____
_____
_____

Day: _____   Date: ___/___/_____

TODAY, I AM GRATEFUL FOR...

_____
_____
_____
_____
_____
_____

AWESOME THINGS THAT HAPPENED TODAY...

_____
_____
_____
_____
_____
_____
_____

Day: _____   Date: ____/____/_____

TODAY, I AM GRATEFUL FOR...

_____

_____

_____

_____

_____

_____

AWESOME THINGS THAT HAPPENED TODAY...

_____

_____

_____

_____

_____

_____

Day: _____   Date: ___/___/_____

TODAY, I AM GRATEFUL FOR...

_____

_____

_____

_____

_____

_____

AWESOME THINGS THAT HAPPENED TODAY...

_____

_____

_____

_____

_____

_____

Day: _____   Date: ___/___/_____

TODAY, I AM GRATEFUL FOR...

_____
_____
_____
_____
_____
_____
_____

AWESOME THINGS THAT HAPPENED TODAY...

_____
_____
_____
_____
_____
_____
_____

Day: _____   Date: ____/____/_____

TODAY, I AM GRATEFUL FOR...

_____

_____

_____

_____

_____

_____

_____

AWESOME THINGS THAT HAPPENED TODAY...

_____

_____

_____

_____

_____

_____

_____

Day: _____   Date: ____/____/_____

TODAY, I AM GRATEFUL FOR...

_____
_____
_____
_____
_____
_____
_____

AWESOME THINGS THAT HAPPENED TODAY...

_____
_____
_____
_____
_____
_____
_____

Day: _____   Date: ___/___/_____

TODAY, I AM GRATEFUL FOR...

_____

_____

_____

_____

_____

_____

AWESOME THINGS THAT HAPPENED TODAY...

_____

_____

_____

_____

_____

_____

_____

Day: _____   Date: ___/___/_____

TODAY, I AM GRATEFUL FOR...

_____
_____
_____
_____
_____
_____
_____

AWESOME THINGS THAT HAPPENED TODAY...

_____
_____
_____
_____
_____
_____

Day: _____   Date: ___/___/_____

TODAY, I AM GRATEFUL FOR...

_____

_____

_____

_____

_____

_____

AWESOME THINGS THAT HAPPENED TODAY...

_____

_____

_____

_____

_____

_____

_____

Day: _____   Date: ____/____/_____

TODAY, I AM GRATEFUL FOR...

_____

_____

_____

_____

_____

_____

_____

AWESOME THINGS THAT HAPPENED TODAY...

_____

_____

_____

_____

_____

_____

_____

Day: _____   Date: ___/___/_____

TODAY, I AM GRATEFUL FOR...

_____

_____

_____

_____

_____

_____

_____

AWESOME THINGS THAT HAPPENED TODAY...

_____

_____

_____

_____

_____

_____

_____

_____

Day: _____   Date: ____/____/_____

TODAY, I AM GRATEFUL FOR...

_____

_____

_____

_____

_____

_____

AWESOME THINGS THAT HAPPENED TODAY...

_____

_____

_____

_____

_____

_____

Day: _____   Date: ___/___/_____

TODAY, I AM GRATEFUL FOR...

_____

_____

_____

_____

_____

_____

AWESOME THINGS THAT HAPPENED TODAY...

_____

_____

_____

_____

_____

_____

_____

_____

Day: _____   Date: ____/____/_____

TODAY, I AM GRATEFUL FOR...

_____

_____

_____

_____

_____

_____

_____

AWESOME THINGS THAT HAPPENED TODAY...

_____

_____

_____

_____

_____

_____

_____

Day: _____   Date: ___/___/_____

TODAY, I AM GRATEFUL FOR...

_____

_____

_____

_____

_____

_____

AWESOME THINGS THAT HAPPENED TODAY...

_____

_____

_____

_____

_____

_____

_____

Day: _____   Date: ____/____/_____

TODAY, I AM GRATEFUL FOR...

_____

_____

_____

_____

_____

_____

AWESOME THINGS THAT HAPPENED TODAY...

_____

_____

_____

_____

_____

_____

Day: _____   Date: ___/___/_____

TODAY, I AM GRATEFUL FOR...

_____

_____

_____

_____

_____

_____

_____

AWESOME THINGS THAT HAPPENED TODAY...

_____

_____

_____

_____

_____

_____

_____

Day: _____   Date: ____/____/_____

TODAY, I AM GRATEFUL FOR...

_____
_____
_____
_____
_____
_____
_____

AWESOME THINGS THAT HAPPENED TODAY...

_____
_____
_____
_____
_____
_____
_____

Day: _____   Date: ___/___/_____

TODAY, I AM GRATEFUL FOR...

_____

_____

_____

_____

_____

_____

AWESOME THINGS THAT HAPPENED TODAY...

_____

_____

_____

_____

_____

_____

_____

Day: _____   Date: ___/___/_____

TODAY, I AM GRATEFUL FOR...

_____
_____
_____
_____
_____
_____
_____
_____

AWESOME THINGS THAT HAPPENED TODAY...

_____
_____
_____
_____
_____
_____
_____
_____

Day: _____   Date: ___/___/_____

TODAY, I AM GRATEFUL FOR...

_____

_____

_____

_____

_____

_____

AWESOME THINGS THAT HAPPENED TODAY...

_____

_____

_____

_____

_____

_____

Day: _____   Date: ___/___/_____

TODAY, I AM GRATEFUL FOR...

_____
_____
_____
_____
_____
_____
_____
_____

AWESOME THINGS THAT HAPPENED TODAY...

_____
_____
_____
_____
_____
_____
_____
_____

Day: _____ Date: ____/____/_____

TODAY, I AM GRATEFUL FOR...

_____
_____
_____
_____
_____
_____
_____

AWESOME THINGS THAT HAPPENED TODAY...

_____
_____
_____
_____
_____
_____
_____

Day: _____   Date: ____/____/_____

TODAY, I AM GRATEFUL FOR...

_____

_____

_____

_____

_____

_____

AWESOME THINGS THAT HAPPENED TODAY...

_____

_____

_____

_____

_____

_____

Day: _____   Date: ____/____/_____

TODAY, I AM GRATEFUL FOR...

_____

_____

_____

_____

_____

_____

AWESOME THINGS THAT HAPPENED TODAY...

_____

_____

_____

_____

_____

_____

Day: _____   Date: ___/___/_____

TODAY, I AM GRATEFUL FOR...

_____

_____

_____

_____

_____

_____

_____

AWESOME THINGS THAT HAPPENED TODAY...

_____

_____

_____

_____

_____

_____

_____

Day: _____   Date: ____/____/_____

TODAY, I AM GRATEFUL FOR...

_____

_____

_____

_____

_____

_____

AWESOME THINGS THAT HAPPENED TODAY...

_____

_____

_____

_____

_____

_____

_____

Day: _____   Date: ___/___/_____

TODAY, I AM GRATEFUL FOR...

_____
_____
_____
_____
_____
_____
_____

AWESOME THINGS THAT HAPPENED TODAY...

_____
_____
_____
_____
_____
_____
_____

Day: _____   Date: ____/____/_____

TODAY, I AM GRATEFUL FOR...

_____

_____

_____

_____

_____

_____

AWESOME THINGS THAT HAPPENED TODAY...

_____

_____

_____

_____

_____

_____

_____

Day: _____   Date: ___/___/_____

TODAY, I AM GRATEFUL FOR...

_____
_____
_____
_____
_____
_____
_____

AWESOME THINGS THAT HAPPENED TODAY...

_____
_____
_____
_____
_____
_____
_____

Day: _____   Date: ___/___/_____

TODAY, I AM GRATEFUL FOR...

_____

_____

_____

_____

_____

_____

AWESOME THINGS THAT HAPPENED TODAY...

_____

_____

_____

_____

_____

_____

Day: _____   Date: ____/____/_____

TODAY, I AM GRATEFUL FOR...

_____

_____

_____

_____

_____

_____

_____

AWESOME THINGS THAT HAPPENED TODAY...

_____

_____

_____

_____

_____

_____

_____

CPSIA information can be obtained
at www.ICGtesting.com
Printed in the USA
LVHW081251180419
614666LV00016B/257/P

9 781976 454493